The Adventures of Javan and the 3 A's

#AsthmaSucks

Written by

Javan Allison
and
Monique Cooper

DEDICATION

Message from Mommy

On February 17, 2018, Javan unexpectedly went from having a simple cough to being admitted into ICU in the hospital. On that day, we were educated on the dos and don'ts of an asthma attack. Most parents and family members of an asthmatic are not aware of how serious this illness can be.

In this book, Javan explains from his own personal experiences how it feels when he is having an asthma attack. A simple cough can be the start of having an asthma attack. We decided to co-write this book to let the world know how a child may feel when he or she cannot breathe. As a mother, my worries go beyond the normal for my child as this illness can be detrimental. I will forever protect Javan from this chronic disease as he lives on to be great.

Javan had a big game coming up. His football team made it to the Little League Super Bowl. Javan was so excited and couldn't wait for the game; but his mom was worried because last night Javan was having trouble breathing.

Javan has asthma, a condition where a person's airways become swollen, narrow, and produces extra mucus which makes it difficult to breathe.

Javan ran to his mommy, "Mommy, I'm super excited for the Super Bowl game! We're going to smash the other team!"

"I'm excited as well, but there won't be a game for you if you're having problems with your asthma," his mommy said.

"But I feel a little better now and by game day I will feel great," Javan said with uncertainty.

"What if you don't?" asked Javan's mom. "Let's remember a time when you were sick. Do Mommy a favor; close your eyes, and let's go on an adventure trip! Tell Mommy how you feel when you have an asthma attack."

Javan then closed his eyes and began to imagine that feeling. As he let his imagination flow, he began to speak about what he remembered.

"I feel like an astronaut flying out of space," said Javan. "In the beginning stages of me coughing, it feels like I'm flying out of space, but I have a crack in my astronaut helmet."

"As I try to get closer to the moon, the coughing gets worse. The crack in my helmet has gotten bigger. There is a pain in my chest as if a small meteor rock hit my helmet and broke it all the way open. Now, I can't breathe at all! The air from outer space has entered into my body and I need oxygen! My stomach hurts from all the coughing. Now, I'm in distress!"

"Ok Javan, open your eyes. Do you want to feel that way again?" asked Javan's mom.

Javan opened his eyes answering, "No mommy, that's not a good feeling. I'm afraid of what can happen next if I can't breathe at all."

"Right! I'm afraid as well. Let's work together to make sure you're taking your medication every day. Be careful during your practices. If you feel like you need a breathing break, let your coaches know, they will understand."

"And then I will be PERFECT for game day!" Javan exclaimed.
"Yes you will," said his mommy.

Game day finally arrived! Javan made a few touchdowns and tackles helping his team win!

Javan ran to his mommy saying, "Mommy, I told you we were going to smash the other team!"
"You sure did! High five!" said his mommy.

Message from Javan

Hi, I'm Javan Allison. I was born earlier than I was supposed to be. At the age of 2-months-old, I started having breathing problems which later gave me severe asthma. Sometimes, I was admitted into ICU in the hospital because I had no air in one of my lungs.

It is important to take care of yourself with this very bad sickness. I know playing with toys and being active is fun, but when you can't breathe and must depend on the hospital's machines, it gets a little annoying. Most asthma attacks start with coughing and wheezing. I have to watch what I eat and watch what I'm around due to me being allergic to some foods, cats, and dogs and more. Those allergens can trigger an asthma attack as well. My mommy and daddy watch me very closely because sometimes I move so fast, I'm not paying attention to myself. So please listen to your body.

S.I.P. Scezare Boles